Active Forgiveness: Freedom to Be a Leader

By: Stan Washington

Overcoming Unforgiveness to Regain Leadership

Active Forgiveness: Freedom to Be a Leader

Printed in the United States of America

First Printing, 2026

ISBN: 978-0-9909831-7-0

Table of Contents

Dedication

This book is dedicated to those who desire to excel, but you feel someone has held you back.

Acknowledgments

Blessed and *honored* are the words that come to mind when it comes to the support I have received. My wife, Gia; daughter, Jasmine; and son, Samuel, have truly hung in there through the thick of things. Thank you. Thanks to my parents who gave me my foundation in CHRIST. Thanks to my big brother Chris and sister-in-law Lisa for doing the heavy lifting when it came to taking care of my parents before they passed away. Thanks to my sister, Linda, who is our family prayer warrior. Thanks to all of my special family and friends who are too numerous to name, who believed in me, encouraged me, and prayed for me. Thank you to all of my clients, customers, and participants for allowing me to serve you all of these years, thus enabling mutual growth.

Stan Washington

Foreword

Achieve success using the GOD-Centered Business Framework (Self-Awareness).

Successful businesses have great solutions to their customer's problems. They also have a leader who can handle dealing with people who bring difficulties into our lives.

Remove the Trash is the Self-Awareness section of the GOD-Centered Business Framework. As a leader, you must be self-aware of anything that is in your heart that could hold you back.

This book will provide leadership tips to grow your resilience to face attackers who may not want you to succeed; even if the attacker is sometimes you.

I will take you on my journey to leadership. **I will ask you challenging questions along the way**. I want you to be a whole leader who can traverse cultural and economic barriers, reaching people with the love that only comes from CHRIST.

Introduction

Just seeing him brought on a landslide of emotions. This guy actively harmed me at every turn he could. Meanwhile he engaged his peers to attack those who supported me. It was a bloody battle in a corporate setting that I was not ready for. All of the leadership training I had taken did not prepare me for blatant disregard for human dignity.

Being caught by surprise happens to the best of us, especially when it comes to a painful experience. It seems like a boss or a business partner, who is supposed to have your best interest in mind, can do some great damage when you were not planning on his or her attack. Does this sound familiar?

During the coercive time, I did not understand what was going on. I received numerous awards for innovation, peer respect and leadership, yet I was being targeted. I would come into the building with a huge smile. I wanted to foster an atmosphere of warmth and togetherness amongst my team. One day my boss secretly said to me "I'm going to wipe that smile off your face." He said it in an even tone, which was scarier than an enraged person.

Being bullied was just the beginning. There was a group of people who did not want to see another group of people succeed. This same boss said to me, "We are going after the leaders who support you." I paraphrased it, because he used names. I have never felt so lonely in my life.

My support was being attacked, I was being attacked and those I supported were being attacked. Nothing seemed fair or good. I feared the worst, and it came true. I was being asked to leave, along with others who supported me. The process of "eliminating" the position would take a while, so I had to work in a hostile environment until my final day. I actually feared for my life as we went on a leadership retreat in a very hot southeast state.

When I made it home, I heard a sermon on the radio. "Forgive your enemies," were the poignant words. Then I heard another sermon on the same thing. "What is GOD trying to say?" I said to myself. I mean, this isn't fair. Bullies who had their five minutes of fame seemed to get their way, meanwhile the people who simply wanted to do a great job were being asked to leave. After hearing yet another speaker express praying for my enemies, I had to take notice. Why was this verse emerging now?

Matthew 5:44 says "*But I say to you, love your enemies, bless those who curse you, do good to those who hate you, and pray for those who spitefully use you and persecute you*"

I also heard another verse. Romans 12:14-21 says "
14 *Bless those who persecute you; bless and do not curse.*
15 *Rejoice with those who rejoice, and weep with those who weep.*
16 *Be of the same mind toward another. Do not set your mind on high things, but associate with the humble. Do not be wise in your own opinion.*

17 *Repay no one evil for evil. Have regard for good things in the sight of all men.*
18 *If it is possible, as much as depends on you, live peaceably with all men.*
19 *Beloved, do not avenge yourselves, but rather give place to wrath; for it is written, "Vengeance is Mine, I will repay," says the Lord.*
20 *Therefore*

"If your enemy is hungry, feed him;
If he is thirsty, give him a drink;
For in so doing you will heap coals of fire on his head."

21 *Do not be overcome by evil, but overcome evil with good.*"

It was actually a relief to pray for my enemies and to forgive those who actively wanted to harm me. For the first time in weeks, I felt inspired to love instead of hating a group of people. Guess what I did. I smiled every day, knowing that this group of people no longer had a hold on my life!

This book will discuss three types of forgiveness:

Active Forgiveness

Reactive Forgiveness

Proactive Forgiveness

Each forgiveness type will be used in different situations you will face during the course of doing business.

You Need This Book If . . .

- You are a small business owner who ran into difficult customers or employees.
- You need a fresh perspective on leading those who surround you to a place of peace.
- You have felt pain caused by someone and are replaying that pain over and over.
- You need to be forgiven, knowing your leadership may be in jeopardy.

Features of This Book

Along with strategies you can use, at the end of each chapter, you'll find one or more of the following bulleted lists:

NEXT STEPS

This section provides three to five tips to implement after you've considered the advice in each chapter.

WARNINGS

In this section, you'll find a list of problems and pitfalls to avoid when executing the items you choose. Each section has specific warnings I collected from my experiences and from other experts to keep you from wasting time and money.

Rotate – Give – Fill Process

Last but not least is our process. Leaders like yourself need a process to forgive people who may be hard to forgive. The Rotate, Give and Fill process will help you regain sleep.

Are they trying to take you off your game?

Is My Leadership Being Stolen?

After playing the hurtful words over in my mind, and walking back through the painful steps, I wanted to tell people how much pain I had experienced. I could see his face in my mind and hear his hurtful words as I sat unemployed, worried about my family's wellbeing.

Loss of Sleep

I lost sleep, and felt enraged about the overt activities this group of people used and had seemingly gotten away with. Meanwhile people who were valued performers were being let go because we looked and acted differently than those in charge. Like me, you may have been robbed of sleep because of what someone else did.

Loss of Sense of Identity

Not only did I lose sleep, I felt a loss of my sense of identity. For years, I stuck my chest out when I told people where I worked and what "my title" was. But then the tables turned. People who once asked me for advice were now avoiding me. I had to do the job as prescribed, until my final day. Then when that day happened and I was on the outside, when people asked me, "what do you do?" I did not have an answer. If you have been hurt, did someone rob you of your sense of identity?

Loss of Trust

My trust in humans was the final thing that was robbed from me. With too much time on my hands, my mind raced, dreaming of all kinds of problems caused by other humans. I would meet strangers who never worked with me, and I would create a wall because they looked and acted similarly to the people who purposefully caused me harm.

I began second-guessing myself by thinking of scenarios of how I worked in the past. I would analyze how I used to handle the situations to make them successful. In my recollection I was rewarded for my actions by some great leaders. But when I did similar actions that once made me successful with great leaders, under this group of poor leaders, my actions were dismissed, ridiculed and twisted.

After this experience of being mistreated and unheard, I recognized the behavior when people behaved similarly, and I would retreat from them. I lost sleep, I lost my sense of identity and I lost my trust.

How Am I Affected?

But what does being robbed of my sleep, my sense of identity and trust have to do with my leadership? **Losing sleep and a sense of identity and not trusting people led me to make decisions from a wounded perspective. This woundedness blinded me from seeing a rich reality that GOD loved and cared for me.** It also blinded me to the fact that GOD loved those who actively hated me.

Before I took the promotion, I was warned that my boss would have a difficult time with someone who looked and acted like me, but I took it as a challenge. But when he got his way and I was let go,

I wanted him to feel the pain I felt. Unfortunately, I got reports that he was doing well during the company restructure. Meanwhile, I was about to walk out the door of a job I was told I was performing well at.

When someone hurts you, it can rob you of many things. **Unforgiveness gives the attacker unnecessary power over your sleep, your sense of identity, joy and trust.** This can show up in your business as you overcompensate by taking on monumental or tiny problems, instead of the ones GOD has assigned to you.

Overcompensation

Do you remember a time when you had mental brakes that would stop you from working twenty-four hours a day, seven days a week? I bet it's a distant memory. This could mean you are trying to show an attacker in your life that you have overcome him or her, versus doing what GOD has called you to do. It could mean you have not forgiven this person. This gives him or her power over you that fuels your actions, and now you are working yourself to exhaustion.

Rushed Decisions

Unforgiveness may also appear in your decisions to hurry up when you should be slowing down to listen to the LORD. Getting a business off the ground can be difficult. Trying to show quick success can possibly lead to a feeling of defeat, which leads to more replaying of the pain the attacker has caused.

Active Forgiveness

That's where **Active Forgiveness** comes in handy. Active Forgiveness is the act of forgiving to regain power that was stolen from you. People say "Forgive and forget" but this makes me more upset, because I cannot seem to forget what happened to me, especially if the event was major in my life. I can't just unhear the words or unsee the activity, or un-feel the bruises.

When JESUS said, "*love your enemies, bless those who curse you, do good to those who hate you, and pray for those who spitefully use you and persecute you,*" I believe HE was helping me regain the power that was stolen from me.

As a leader, it may be difficult for you to be above the situation if you keep replaying things that wounded you. I do not believe JESUS is saying "Stay with abusive people" or "Hang in there because I will not help."

My first observation of what JESUS said is, "Love your enemies." This lets us know that we will have enemies who may be influenced by their own sin nature. Trying to control this human will only make us lose sleep, lose our sense of identity and lose trust in people. We will ultimately lose our joy.

Recognizing that some people will actively engage in their sin, helps you to not be surprised when leaders try to actively harm people. It does not make their action right, but it does prepare you to stand guard. **When** someone tries to harm you, you will not be surprised. It gives you back your sleep because you expected the attack.

JESUS said in Matthew 10:16

"Behold, I send you out as sheep in the midst of wolves. Therefore be wise as serpents and harmless as doves."

This means you need to understand that some people will not have your best interest in mind, but you do not have to act like them.

JESUS was mistreated, despised and hated. HE doesn't invite us to misery, but to HIS victory. HE has been on the other side of death, and now that HE is raised from the dead, HIS words become more powerful than ever.

"Do I have to tell the person 'I forgive you'?" you may ask.

If the person asks for forgiveness, yes. But if they have not asked for forgiveness, their harm should not hold you back from releasing them. You can forgive a person without saying it in this instance.

forgive - stop feeling angry or resentful toward (someone) for an offense, flaw, or mistake. – cancel a debt.

Reactive Forgiveness

It takes time for your wounds to heal. Let's be honest, if you are around the person who caused the original pain long enough, then you may eventually experience more pain. Then it compounds the pain you originally felt. This is where **Reactive Forgiveness** comes in. Reactive Forgiveness gives you back your brakes on your tongue. When you want to say something to combat what the harmful person said, GOD helps you to be quiet long enough to think about your response. "Is my response in love or pain?" "Do I actually love this person as GOD loves him or her?" "Should I even respond to this statement or can I let it go?" These are great questions to ask yourself before you respond. What other questions can you think of?

In James 3:4-11 it says:

"4 Look also at ships: although they are so large and are driven by fierce winds, they are turned by a very small rudder wherever the pilot desires. 5 Even so the tongue is a little member and boasts great things.

See how great a forest a little fire kindles! 6 And the tongue is a fire, a world of iniquity. The tongue is so set among our members that it defiles the whole body, and sets on fire the course of nature; and it is set on fire by hell. 7 For every kind of beast and bird, of reptile and creature of the sea, is tamed and has been tamed by mankind. 8 But no man can tame the tongue. It is an unruly evil, full of deadly poison. 9 With it we bless our God and Father, and with it we curse men, who have been made in the similitude of God. 10 Out of the same mouth proceed blessing and cursing. My brethren, these things ought not to be so. 11 Does a spring send forth fresh water and bitter from the same opening?

I have said this before many times "It's not the situation; it's how you **respond** to the situation that makes or breaks you. Reactive Forgiveness tells you to "Be quiet and **respond well**."

When you are frustrated, you may have to step away from the situation to develop a response that does not curse the person because in doing so, you not only hurt them, you hurt yourself.

Blessing a person who has cursed you actually heals you. As a leader, your first reaction is important. If you react with the same hatred or ignorance a person is placing on you, it drags you down. Reactive Forgiveness makes you think, "What is the best outcome for both of us?"

Proactive Forgiveness

But what happens when you know you are about to enter a place where the people have a reputation of being combative, disruptive or evil, and you still have to go there? The feeling that "I have to lose" may come flooding back as you start replaying old recordings stored up in your mind from previous wounds.

Not this time! **Proactive Forgiveness** is the act of forgiving a type of person who reminds you of the one who caused you harm.

JESUS said in Luke 23:34

"Father, forgive them, for they do not know what they do."

I believe HE was giving you and me the power to execute Proactive Forgiveness. HE was about to be crucified, but it had not happened yet. HE was about to be stripped of HIS clothes, yet HE asked the FATHER to forgive them before it happened.

Proactive Forgiveness does the same thing. Instead of acquiescing to the potential bullies, it makes you pray ahead of time, asking the LORD for strength, wisdom and a heart of forgiveness.

Bullies, bullies, bullies, bullies, bullies all around!

Shaping of My Leadership

Weighing 108 pounds at five feet, ten inches did not seem flattering to the women at my high school. But that wasn't the only thing I obsessed over. In elementary school, I had ill fitting, torn-up clothes, and professor-rimmed glasses. Unfortunately, my clothes and glasses were not the trend at the time. To top it off, I had nappy hair.

Self-Perception

Getting teased was the norm for me. I was called names like "Captain Naps" and "BB King" and "Nap King Cole." This was before the current hair styles. People would tell me to comb my hair, but they did not realize that I had done so. It would get nappy an hour after I combed it. My siblings were away at college and my parents worked around the clock just to make ends meet. I did not have anyone at home to help me dress or groom. I did not know this was shaping me as a leader.

I looked in the mirror, pulled out my pick and tried to straighten my hair. It was super tangled and hurt with every pull. I got a brilliant idea. I would wet it to ease the strokes. Little did I know that wetting my hair would cause it to knot up even more when it dried out.

> Leadership Tip #1 – The enemy wants to distract you from your GOD-given purpose.

On the playground in elementary school, people would loop their finger and thumb around my wrist to demonstrate how skinny I was, as if I didn't know! I have no idea why, but my clothes also became a subject of ridicule. I did not know this was shaping me as a leader as well.

Fortunately for me, I still made friends. They lived on different blocks in the city. My neighborhood was all one race and most households had three kids for some reason. Later in life I found out that my parents were not allowed to purchase property in certain neighborhoods. **Everyone in my neighborhood looked like me**. Did everyone look like you, where you grew up? I did not notice anything wrong with where I grew up.

Avoiding Bullies Doesn't Always Work

But I did notice the bullies. On my way to school, I had to create a route that would avoid certain households. Most of the parents in my neighborhood were hard working. But there was always one house on every block that had a wild family living there. Every now and then, I would be confronted by a bully. They would ask intimidating questions, catching me off guard. They would threaten me, but I had no money at the time, so they would leave me alone. Once again, I did not know this was shaping me as a leader.

To avoid getting beat up, I formed a plan. I would leave my house early, walk out of my way to go to one of my best friend's house, then I would walk to school with him because I felt there was strength in numbers. It worked, most of the time. But sometimes they would get both of us. Are you trying to avoid people so you won't get hurt again?

Adding CHRIST as the Answer

Being teased made me want a relationship with someone who wanted me for me. My mother was my Sunday School teacher. She taught me about CHRIST. She said, "HE will accept you just as you are." **I did not like who I was**, but thought it would be great to be loved without worry of being ridiculed. I accepted CHRIST at the age of 12. I thought life would be so easy if I just had CHRIST in my life!

My father moved back into the house after moving out. I was alone with my mother for a while and had to learn how to take care of a house while taking care of her during her bought with cancer. I would listen to the radio stations she listened to. She loved Christian radio and I became accustomed to it. This affected my leadership.

Labels Affected Me

I was labeled as "smart," not because I was smart, but because I wore professor-rimmed glasses. Even the teachers believed I was smart, so I started believing it too! I excelled in math and took high school math in eighth grade. When the high schoolers yelled "Freshies" to us, we giggled, knowing that we were eighth graders! I took a placement test to go to the same school that my siblings attended. Lindblom Technical High School only allowed students who could pass the entrance exam. I passed!

But then I got to high school. The bullies got bigger and more numerous. I was robbed on a public bus once. My best friend and I were chased by several gang members more than once. One said "Pull out your gun and shoot him," as we zig zagged in our sprint away from them. We were on the track team and they could not get close! Do you feel bullied because someone mislabeled you?

It Was a Struggle

Lindblom students from my neighborhood had to travel more than an hour to get to school, traveling through many difficult territories on public transportation. My morning commute took planning. I had to get up at 5 AM to shower and dress to make it on the 5:25 bus, two blocks away. If I missed that bus, the connecting bus was one mile away! The connecting bus after that was five miles away.

Every now and then I would miss the first bus and had to run with a backpack full of books, to the connecting bus. I enjoyed empty buses. No thugs, and empty seats meant I could get a 5-minute nap. I traveled from Maple Park to Englewood. This took four buses. I spent so much time on buses that I could get my homework done. I did not know this would shape my leadership. Are you seeing a pattern?

No Money

My father would give me $7.50 to ride the bus to school, eat lunch and ride the bus back home. Yes, this pricing seems ancient but it has relevance. He would actually count the money out in quarters. If I would lose one quarter, I could not eat that day. Lunch was fifty cents and so were the back-and-forth bus rides. This would shape my financial leadership.

I was getting nowhere when it came to clothes and glasses. I got a job at a bowling alley making $3.10 an hour. I got a raise when minimum wage went up to $3.35 an hour. I worked weekends. On Friday I worked from 6:00 PM to 2:00 AM and Saturday's I worked from 5:00 PM to 3:00 AM. I was making $60 a week and my expenses were $7.50! I was rich!

I bought clothes, glasses and went to the barber shop regularly. "The girls will have to love me now," I thought. But to my dismay, they said, "You are too skinny!" My efforts to fit in failed. Do you feel like you don't fit in?

Brief Glimpse of a Calling

One day at lunch, a good friend brought someone over to me. He was a junior and I was a sophomore. The guy began asking questions about CHRIST in a disbelieving manner. Strangely, I was able to answer the questions well enough that the person stopped questioning and said, "you answered well." This shaped my godly leadership.

No Help. No Direction.

"What school are you going to apply to?" was the foreign question posed to me. My best friend said he was going to apply to the University of Illinois Champaign, Urbana. Throughout high school, I was put in advanced placement (AP) classes. I did well in AP English, AP Physics and Calculus. One of my teachers asked me if I would enroll in her computer class when I was going into my senior year. I didn't even know what a computer was! I took the class and fell in love with technology. On the **one** application I filled out for college, I asked to become a Computer Science major. I was accepted into U of I.

My parents could not help me because they had not gone to college. My mom became a nurse through a manpower program. She had tests and a certification she had to pass, but not from a 4-year university. My dad was a printer and a mechanic who had a gas station at one point, but worked on cars in our garage.

I went to college. I bought a car from my father for $200. My sister and I went Christmas shopping in the car. I hit a patch of ice and slammed into a light pole. Her head hit the windshield but she was alright. My father, being a mechanic, was able to repair it to a point. But now the fender and hood were bent and the car was actually dangerous to drive, because it would lurch forward when I used the brakes.

After getting off work from my janitor job, I was driving with my best friend to go to my fraternity's party. Yes, we went to the same college. In fact, we went to grammar school, high school, college and pledged Alpha Phi Alpha together. While driving around our apartment, another student turned left in front of me. We were both bad drivers, but he was a worse driver. My car was totaled, but we were fine. This shaped my leadership.

Harm for No Reason

As I walked down the hallway of my dorm one day, a guy stuck his head out of a room. "Hey n****r!" was his statement. I immediately was enraged! I was being bullied by someone who did not look like me. I told my best friend and I found a friend who was the night clerk and six feet three inches, weighing over three hundred pounds.

We banged on the door. When they finally opened it, there was a group of guys in there who also did not look like me. "Which one used a racial slur?" was the night clerk's question to me. I went over to the guy and pushed his forehead with my fingers, saying "this one!" The night clerk warned the guys, then he punched their loft that was a makeshift bunkbed. It broke. The visitor who yelled out the door said nothing. The next day, the entire floor had to meet to discuss racial sensitivity.

"Are you kidding me!? I have been bullied by people who look like me and now I am bullied by people who don't look like me," I thought to myself. This shaped my leadership.

Hypocrites!

I wanted to be away from my parents. I saw their Christianity and somehow applied the label of failure on them, when in reality, I just wanted to experience the world without their rules. I did not want to go home during the summers, rather I wanted to experience the things they told me not to do. I stopped going to church, had sex, got drunk and had a "good" time. If you have been mislabeled, are you mislabeling someone as a hypocrite?

My roommate and I once counted twenty-two phone calls, in ten minutes, asking if we were going to hold a party that night. We had taken the weekend off. I got so involved with enjoying myself, that I lost track of my studies. I was thrown out of college. I talked myself back into college and eventually graduated. This shaped my leadership.

Unforgiveness blinds the senses. Sight decreases. Hearing goes away. Smells increase. Taste gets bitter, touch becomes numb and hearing shuts off.

I cannot **see** the other person's perspective, **hear** what they are trying to say, **taste** any good message from them. I can **smell** something is fishy. And I lose **touch** with my purpose in GOD.

I **hear** words that are not said, and remember those I choose to remember. I **see** faults but cannot see fixes. My **touch** is with a fist. My **taste** is bitter and salty. Everything **stinks**! **Unforgiveness, you have stolen from me your last time!**

Am I cut out to be a leader?

GOD Made Me a Leader

Applying to only **one** college worked out well for me. I went to the school I applied to and took the **one** suit I owned that I graduated from high school in. I applied to multiple jobs but received **one** offer away from my home state. Upon arrival in the small town, I tried prayer. I hadn't prayed or attended church in a long time, but I figured I would give it a shot. I asked GOD for an apartment. I drove around and about 10 minutes into the search, I found an apartment that was extremely close to work. Google did not exist.

"Wow! That worked out." I thought to myself. Weeks later I brought my stuff packed in the trunk of my car. I moved in within ten minutes. The company I worked for paid for a hotel while I had furniture delivered. I was a programmer and was paid better than I had ever been paid before. This time I was making $12.50 an hour! That was double what I was making as a janitor in college!

I went grocery shopping and bought a 64-ounce can of juice. Does juice even come in cans that size anymore? Anyway, I bought the juice along with bread and lunchmeat. I sat down to eat and realized I didn't have a can opener. I got angry at my parents for that.

Leadership Tip #2 – GOD made situations, gifts and talents to make you a great leader!

Angry and Frustrated

I had no one to guide me to go to college or through college and now I was in this dinky little town, alone! I was mad that I had to make every decision alone! That night I prayed for a second time. This time my prayer was simple. “LORD, please make me successful.” That was it. I went to bed. I had no idea what GOD had in store for me.

I wrote code for portions of the 911 system for a very large company. I was paid well, but I wanted to get out of tech and into the business-side of business. I looked for a job to no avail. **I felt stuck**. I decided that I would go to church. After visiting a few churches, I made the statement “Church is useless!” I then said, “All of the pastors are after women and money” as if that wasn’t what I sought after. Have you ever gotten mad at GOD? We all have.

Maybe Clubs Will Cure My Loneliness

I stopped going to church again out of frustration, but my loneliness kicked in. *I would learn later that frustrated decision making would get me in more trouble than I would expect.* I met people at work and went to clubs with them. I got into bodybuilding to address the “skinny” problem I had been dealing with all my life. I wanted to look good at the clubs. It worked! I was six feet tall and muscular. Coming in from exercising, an “old” woman in my apartment building met me at the door and asked me the strangest question, “Where do you go to church?” She was ancient, maybe in her late fifties! I was in my mid twenties.

She told me to try a church she used to go to. I went and heard the preacher speak about the book of Revelation. As a child, the pastor of the church I attended told me not to read the book of

Revelation because I would not understand it. This made me more curious about reading it.

I joined that church and the desire came up inside me to become a Sunday School teacher, like my parents. I did so. But on Saturdays, I would go out and "have fun." I refrained from drinking as much, but every now and then I would drink more than usual. I would let my inhibitions down.

One Sunday I was walking downstairs with my Sunday School class and heard a guy call my attention by saying directly to me, "We had fun with the women at the Firehouse last night!" The Firehouse was a dance and mingle club that I wanted to keep secret from my class. GOD didn't shame me; I was ashamed because I didn't know HIS true grace. My club friends gave me misinformation that I had to be sinless to have a relationship with CHRIST. I was taught otherwise, but wanting to fit in, I believed them and was willing to not learn about GOD.

But something stirred in my heart. I decided to stop going to clubs and to concentrate on my Bible study to cure my boredom. I even gave up drinking because of what I was willing to do while drunk. A few months later, I got a job offer for a position I did not apply to. A recruiter called me, saying she heard about me.

A New Job

I started working for a company back in my hometown that specialized in consulting CEOs, CMOs, CFOs and other officers in the "C" suite. I learned from them and became more and more polished in my corporate speech. I decided to use some of it on my dad. I asked him why he left and came back. I did not get a good answer, but I was able to say,"I forgive you." It felt weird and I felt I had grown up. I wanted a father and was not going to have one by trying to change him. The change would need to come from within.

I got married and two years later, our first child was on the way. I just finished attending a Bible School and had joined a church. Life couldn't be better! But I was traveling a lot. I prayed and asked GOD for a job that would keep me local. Shortly after our first child was born, I got wind of a position at a large company that would keep me local. I applied and got an offer from the company that paid a couple of thousand less than I was making at the consulting firm. It was still double my first salary!

At the previous two companies, I was not promoted, even though I asked. **I got frustrated** at both companies. I went into this new company with an attitude that this would be the best job I ever had! My first evaluation was from a person who came into the company after me and was hired in as my boss. He quickly got a reputation for making men and women cry, literally.

He evaluated me as "good" which was a step above "needs improvement." Meanwhile, I was probably working fifty to sixty hours a week. I later found out that the working long hours did not matter, it was the relationships that helped with promotions.

Leadership Traits I Was Taught

I took a leadership development class that put a few missing pieces in place for me.

1. I needed to **think strategically** instead of tactically.
2. I was in **control of the pace**.
3. I needed to **get rid of any rage** and **think like a team**, no matter who was on the team.
4. The **company was my number one priority**.

The last one is not GOD-Centered.

I took this class to heart and was promoted for the first time. I thought it was my performance, but it wasn't. A friend from my old high school worked at the same company. He and I started a Bible study that was multiethnic. A Senior Vice President got wind of my belief in CHRIST and was watching over me. He urged the promotion because he believed in CHRIST. GOD was intervening in my path.

Life-Changing Decision

The pastor at the church I attended invited me to go on a mission trip to Zimbabwe. I was already doing street witnessing around the church and felt no need to leave the country. But GOD moved my heart and I accepted.

When the pastor and I went out street witnessing around the church, an incarcerated guy accepted CHRIST as his LORD and Savior. Prior to the mission trip, I went back to visit him, only to find out he had been shot to death. This made me serious about the mission of the trip.

In Zimbabwe, our hired van broke down at a major bus stop. The city of Harare reminded me of Atlanta, with tall buildings, banks and traffic. I got out and did street witnessing. I met a man and asked him if he wanted me to pray for him. His eyes were yellowish red. He said yes. I prayed with him and we talked about the love of CHRIST. I told him I used to drink. He didn't believe that his eyes could clear up as clear as mine were.

He accepted CHRIST and brought his mother and wife over to hear the Gospel. They also accepted CHRIST. This set me on fire! Later, I met a man in a hut while on the same trip. We had to leave the city to see him. He had a lemon tree, some chickens and a cow. He sat outside of the hut talking to me.

He expressed the pride he had in these possessions, not knowing about computers, electricity, appliances or any of the problems the things I had would cause. His contentment was amazing to me.

This trip was life-changing! I saw leadership differently. GOD showed me that I was supposed to be a **servant leader** versus a tyrant or a snake, like I was being taught.

When I returned to the United States, I was promoted a few more times. Our second child was born. I was sent out west to take over from a leader who was being let go from the company in the restructure. During this time, I served under a very prominent speaker who traversed races and filled stadiums with the Gospel of CHRIST.

I found my purpose in life, namely to serve CHRIST. I opened my home to people who accepted CHRIST after the event. I was willing to stay in this town forever, but we moved back to the Midwest for family desires. I was promoted again; this time I was over Operations and Technology for the nation. I was headed back into a hostile environment at headquarters.

You would think that I had to learn something special to be put in this position of responsibility, but it was the things I learned along the way that made me successful. Let's take a look.

Leadership Lessons from Childhood (**True Differentiators**)

Remember I told you I was teased about my hair, clothes and body shape? **As a leader I recognized that there was no place for hateful, negative language**. I even removed talking about people's skin color, hair types and clothing from my vocabulary. This reduced my discussions about celebrities as my idols.

As a child, I was labeled as "smart" because of my professor-rimmed glasses. I became "smart" because I believed the label. If a positive label could transform me this much, imagine the damage a negative label will have on someone. **I encouraged people to use their gifts.**

I saw people who were overlooked by other leaders due to quick judgment. It took more patience, but **I was able to build people up so they could excel.** This behavior spilled into my personal life. One time, I served at a homeless shelter and rode in the van they used to pick the regulars up and brought them back to the shelter. "Look, there's one of ours," the driver said. "Where?" I replied. When we got closer, **I could see the invisible people** sitting outside in plain view. This happened after I left the large company, but it fits here in my leadership recap.

I traded in my gossip language for encouraging my team. When I ran into corporate bullies, I was able to talk with them versus getting mad at them and fighting them. I took lessons from when I was 108 pounds and had to learn how to persuade people versus fighting. **I learned how to influence them by finding common ground**, even if I did not agree with them.

Remember that homework I did on the bus? **I learned to work off kilter** and was able to get things done without needing the perfect conditions. Working on the bus made me **learn how to use time management** to get my homework out, done and put away before I had to get off the bus.

Or how about that $7.50 I had to manage? **I learned how to budget, control spending, invest, and make payments when needed. I learned how to be generous** at the right time. I began giving in church and directly to people. I also learned to keep my expense reports immaculate. I never charged the company more than a meal I purchased and made my travel modestly.

From the difficult experiences, **I learned how to hold my tongue versus blurting out my emotional response**. This came in handy when it came to negotiations, and budget debates.

Talking my way back in school required that I **acknowledge the situation, develop a plan and convince those in charge that the plan was feasible by showing steps**.

Peers would dismiss people in corporate settings, judging them by their hair and clothes. But **I could see potential in people** that others could not see. GOD had me **treat all people as equal**. **I worked from a place of gratitude** and saw my large team thrive. They were excited and were doing more than they had ever done before.

The mission trips shaped my belief in GOD further. Seeing how people lived around the world was humbling. **I humbly reduced the demands I had and became content with life, but became an advocate for people. I also learned to put my trust in GOD more and more.**

Being robbed and bullied shaped me to **be generous and to help people** with their careers versus trying harm them. **I wanted people to achieve more than I could achieve and to outgrow me**. I did not need people to make me famous because **I was busy making others famous**.

I found that my past difficult experiences were actually helping me versus holding me back. My peers seemed to come from privileged backgrounds and could not come up with the ideas that I had because they did not come from difficult times. Their entire existence was supported by who they knew. If someone who supported them left, they would have to leave too.

I discovered that true leadership is not about being above people or even being better than people; rather it is about loving CHRIST and serving people to make them better to serve GOD wholeheartedly.

I was on top of my game. How could life get any better than this? But in my heart, I was becoming miserable. Dealing with one corporate bully is easy, but after a dozen, the energy got old.

I was given a company luxury car. One day, I sat in the car, trying to figure out how to leave "me" in the car and become who "they" wanted me to be. I missed the old me. I no longer held Bible studies or spoke much about CHRIST. I was a corporate leader.

Next-level thinking needs me to be above it all.

How Active Forgiveness Heals Me

Being in leadership meant I was in a coveted position. I never knew the position I held could be coveted by my boss. When the position I held was eliminated, he had to do my work. This news did not cheer me up. After telling people about my pain, I felt great because people were sympathetic and empathetic. But I found myself telling the story over and over. Then, one day, I noticed less sympathy and less empathy. I realized I was stuck! The pain the person caused me was very real, but it also caused me to be stuck in a moment in time that I would replay if anyone would listen.

Active Forgiveness is the <u>repetitious</u> and <u>perpetual</u> act of intentionally forgiving an attacker with the goal of releasing the negative power they seem to hold over you and to release bitterness you may have acquired that could harm you and people around you.

Over time bitterness can creep into your heart, which can affect your thoughts, and ultimately affect your decisions. Soon, you may think of ways to harm yourself and others. Peter asked JESUS a very important question which JESUS gave a strange response. Matthew 18:21-22 –

"[21] Then Peter came to Him and said, "Lord, how often shall my brother sin against me, and I forgive him? Up to seven times?"

Leadership Tip #3 – Healed people heal people.

[22] Jesus said to him, "I do not say to you, up to seven times, but up to seventy times seven."

I believe Peter was trying to double what church leaders called Pharisees taught in terms of forgiveness. They would say forgive three times based on the prophet Amos. I suggest you read Amos chapter 1 to understand where Pharisees got this belief. I believe Peter not only wanted to double the number, but throw in one extra. JESUS blew his number away by saying, "*seventy times seven,*" or a number that would make you stop counting because you can't keep track of the same offense. HE also knew it would take time, and repetition to build up resilience from attackers.

In Psalm 103:12 –

"*[12] As far as the east is from the west,*
So far has He removed our transgressions from us."

GOD tells us that HE does not even remember your sins when HE removes them. HIS example of removing the sin is to **restore the person who wants to be restored.** Not every attacker will want your forgiveness, but those who seek it should be restored.

Active Forgiveness is not for the person who hurt you, it's for you! Staying wounded is a dangerous place to remain. It could mean "they won" and "you lost." You cannot have this happen. In order for both of you to win in this situation, GOD gives us a way, namely to forgive. When you forgive someone, you win GOD's heart. **GOD uses the repetitious part of Active Forgiveness on you every day**. HE only has love for you and holds no bitterness.

It took a while for me to pray for my enemies, but, over time, it did release my anger. I could actually feel the power my attacker had over me dissipate. In fact, I started seeing other people who acted just like my attacker as people GOD loves and wants them to be saved.

Wanting the BEST for People

I no longer wanted harm to befall this person, rather, I wanted the best for him. What? You wanted the BEST? Yes! JESUS gave us this instruction in Matthew 7:12 –

"So in everything, do to others what you would have them do to you, for this sums up the Law and the Prophets."

And Solomon wrote in Proverbs 11:25 –

[25] *A generous person will prosper;*
whoever refreshes others will be refreshed.

It is also written in Proverbs 11:27 –

"He who earnestly seeks good finds favor, But trouble will come to him who seeks evil."

Let's be real; when I want harm to fall on someone, it is evil. I am usually not thinking of GOD or the other person. I want him or her to fail and fail miserably.

This kind of attitude can cause me to be stuck, waiting on them to fail and when they don't, I feel more pain.

GOD gave us great words of advice through Paul in Romans 12:17- 21 –

"[17] Repay no one evil for evil. Have regard for good things in
the sight of all men. [18] If it is possible, as much as depends on
you, live peaceably with all men. [19] Beloved, do not avenge
yourselves, but rather give place to wrath; for it is
written, "Vengeance is Mine, I will repay," says the
Lord. [20] Therefore

"If your enemy is hungry, feed him;
If he is thirsty, give him a drink;
For in so doing you will heap coals of fire on his head."

[21] *Do not be overcome by evil, but overcome evil with good."*

Observation 1: No evil for evil.

GOD says a mouthful in the passages of Scripture listed above. Here are a few of my observations. First **GOD tells me to not repay evil for evil**, even though this was the common practice was from the Levitical Law as seen in Leviticus 24:19-20 –

"19 'If a man causes disfigurement of his neighbor, as he has done, so shall it be done to him— 20 fracture for fracture, eye for eye, tooth for tooth; as he has caused disfigurement of a man, so shall it be done to him.'" JESUS wants us to show the power of mercy.

Mercy means you have the power to judge or persecute someone and choose not to. Will you add mercy to your leadership?

Observation 2: People are always watching my response.

The second thing I see is, **people are watching my response**. When GOD inspired Paul to write "*Have regard for good things in the sight of all men*" and "*live peaceably with all men,*" HE is telling me that **my life is HIS** and I am supposed to be HIS example. I do not think HE is telling me to "suck it up, you big baby!" I really believe HE is trying to help me regain my sleep and my sense of identity and my trust that was stolen.

When I live in peace in front of those who cause me harm, I sleep well! I mean, I sleep so well, that I feel like I do not have a care. This brings a smile to my face that should not be there. My enemies see me smiling and may wonder why. The evil they try to pour out on me falls back on them. Do you feel you are an ambassador for GOD who is protected?

Observation 3: Revenge is not mine.

The last thing I see in the passage Paul wrote is to **stay away from revenge.** When I take revenge on my enemy, I am actually stealing from GOD. HE said, "*Vengeance is Mine, I will repay.*" This clearly says who owns the vengeance. When I take vengeance, passively or aggressively, GOD sees me doing it and now I have a problem with the person I am retaliating on and I have a problem with GOD. I end up in worse shape.

I will paraphrase what I think GOD told Adam and Eve in the book of Genesis, "These two trees are MINE. Do not eat from the Tree of Knowledge and the Tree of Life." When they ate from the Tree of Knowledge, all of humanity fell. Similarly, I believe HE means it when HE says "*Vengeance is Mine, I will repay.*" The Tree is HIS and the vengeance is HIS. This should not be taken lightly.

GOD gave us some guidelines HE wants us to follow. By performing Active Forgiveness, we can feed a hungry enemy and give him something to drink. GOD says, "*you will heap coals of fire on his head.*"

Wanting the best for people also means I want the best for myself. Wanting harm to fall on someone means I want harm to fall on me. It's just that simple. I choose to want the best, even for my enemies, and leave it up to GOD when that person follows HIM or not.

To be honest, sometimes I ask GOD, "Did YOU see that?" as if HE didn't see or hear what my enemy said or did. HE sees their action, but HE also sees my response. Active Forgiveness helps you forgive your enemy, be above the situation and to look great in front of other humans. Can you let go of revenge and allow GOD to have it?

WARNING

- Recognize that some people are trying to keep you from being the best version of yourself GOD wants you to be.
- Steer clear of overworking. Develop definitive start and stop times that are comfortable for work/ life balance.
- Do not let too much time go past without reconciling with people. Is this the problem that ends the relationship? What does GOD have to say about this relationship?
- Be wise enough to give people space, especially if they have abusive tendencies towards you.

NEXT STEPS

- Forgive them.
- Take a moment to think about who hurt you, what they did and why it still hurts. This may or may not include the people you thought you had reconciled with and moved on. Think of the person or people you still need to forgive. Maybe the person you need to forgive is yourself.
- Write who hurt you. On a separate sheet of paper, write out what the person did and how it made you feel.
- This may not be easy right now, especially if the wound is still fresh. Start a prayer that begins with "I accept the power of love by forgiving myself and them for hurting me." Add additional words. Tear up the paper to release the person.

Active Forgiveness
Freedom to Be a Leader

We all have to win. When one person loses, we all lose.

Reactive Forgiveness Becomes My First Response

I really wanted to confront my attacker to convince him how foolish his attacks were, but it never happened. This left me in a state of desiring to win, but having no way to do it. It also left me wounded and I found myself insecure, trying to convince people "I am right" versus exploring other possibilities in alternatives presented to me or simply just being right without having to convince other people.

Whenever a person was "wrong," I quickly wanted to point out the problem with his or her statement. My first response to their statement needed to change.

Reactive Forgiveness is the act of <u>slowing down</u> to think of a response that enables you and your attacker to win in GOD's eyes, while intentionally bringing peace to potential combative situations.

Wanting to win showed up in my business. Customers had to lose in order for me to win, according to what I was taught. I learned from salespeople to understand the pain points that customers have, magnify those pain points, and to develop a pitch to convince him or her that my product or service was the answer. Unfortunately, at the time, I was not convinced that my product or service was an answer to anyone's problem except my own, namely needing to get paid!

Leadership Tip #4 – Listening is the leader's best tool. Ask questions and listen more.

Unforgiveness Made Me Desperate

In my desperation, I tried to mimic successful people or meet successful people or beg successful people to help me. Instead of losing my sense of identity to a bad boss, this time I was losing it to my business. I wanted to win so badly that I would sell all the time, wherever I went. I became disappointed in family and friends for not supporting the business.

I then became defensive about my business, especially when confronted about something that was not complete or something that was not working. My frustration was the first thing out of my mouth. It felt good to tell people about my frustrations, but it left a terrible first impression on potential customers who I did not know were watching me. Are you venting frustrations in a stuck fashion?

First Impressions Are Forever

First impressions can never happen again. Don't get me wrong, perceptions about you can change, but I am talking about the very first impression will always be the first. When you speak to someone, you should desire to speak to him or her again. A negative first impression may inhibit that desire to continue a relationship with you in the recipient.

Do you get mad, enraged, and visibly upset at people and later have to apologize? Your first impression may be that of an angry person.

But what if the person you are working with has just said something that is blatantly meant to harm you? GOD wants you to respond with **Reactive Forgiveness**.

Talking Intentionally

Taming your tongue means you plan on making a good first impression. It also means thinking out your responses before you say them. Many times I do not need to respond because I would say something that would get me in trouble with GOD. Lastly, I had to examine my motives to see if I wanted to hurt the person or heal our relationship.

I believe GOD despises when you and I curse someone, no matter how wicked the person is. I also believe that Satan is an accuser. He tricked humans to fall by lying to Eve. He then made Adam insecure, causing him to blame Eve and blame GOD for making Eve.

Satan was one of the most beautiful of all angels. Instead of putting the entire chapter in this book, I suggest you read see Ezekiel 28. His pride made him fall. Now he wants you and me to do his dirty work. He wants us to become combative and accusatory. I suggest you read 2 Corinthians 11. He knows he cannot be in multiple places at once like GOD. He therefore needs us to do the accusing, blaming and fighting for him.

One way he does this is to make our response negative when it comes to passive jabs thrown at us, overt name calling hitting us and slanderous words, filled with his poison, slicing us. He wants us to behave like him instead of having a tamed tongue.

In the *GOD-Centered Business: A Foundational Framework to Grow with Resilience*, it states to "Remove the Trash" from our hearts. The trash represents negative blockers that reside in our hearts that cause us to lie, cheat and steal, for example. Removing the Trash requires that I respond to people who try to harm me, with love, joy, peace, patience, kindness, goodness, faithfulness, gentleness and self-control. This is known as the Fruit of the Spirit.

You Will Always Respond with Your Heart

You are always going to respond with what is in your heart. If pain, hurt, misery, bitterness, shame or rage are in your heart, you will respond with them. Your first response will come out in frustration, rage or you may be silent, not in a good way.

What? A silent person can be filled with rage? Yes. While quieting down is a good practice, being willing to never speak to people again may be a terrible practice. Are you easily enraged and willing to never speak to people again?

Responding Well

Reactive Forgiveness helps you to **quiet down to think of a response that would enable everyone to win.** Your customers will appreciate winning and so will you. But GOD has to show you where you can help your attacker feel like they are part of HIS family, if it is your place to do so. This takes discernment.

I do understand that putting some boundaries between some people is healthy. As stated before, you do not have to remain around bullies (passive or overt). But GOD doesn't want us to constantly run away from people who do not look or think like us. HE wants us to work out differences as best we can. HE wants you to **be the one who brings HIS peace to the situation.**

Reactive Forgiveness helps you plan out your responses to bring peace to the conversation. You cannot remain silent forever, waiting on him or her to reach out to you. You must **collect yourself enough to calmly express the pain** to your attacker, at the same time, seeking this person to have GOD's best.

"**I have to let go of this!**" is a great statement to say to yourself. Whatever pain or problem you are holding onto will definitely hold you back from growing up. It may feel comfortable to hold onto pain, and people may enable you to feel sorry for yourself, but GOD wants to heal your wounds. This requires that you let the situation go and possibly the person.

Taming My Tongue

Wanting to control the attacker is a mistake we all make. We want peace, but have a limiting belief that if I am heard by the attacker, then peace can be achieved. This only works when the attacker is whole and can hear you. But there may be those who do not wish to hear you. Will you have your peace robbed from you?

Trying to control the attacker could make us accidentally want to respond quickly, emotionally and sometimes loudly. Ask yourself, "**Is this conversation going to rob me or that person from having peace?**" You have to be honest with yourself when checking to see if you want to win versus keeping your peace.

James said the tongue is small like a rudder, but powerful because it can praise GOD and curse humans who were made in HIS image. Read James chapter 3. But GOD spoke through James in this passage:

James 1: 1:19 *My dear brothers and sisters, take note of this: Everyone should be quick to listen, slow to speak and slow to become angry,*

22 But be doers of the word, and not hearers only, deceiving yourselves. 23 For if anyone is a hearer of the word and not a doer, he is like a man observing his natural face in a mirror; 24 for he observes himself, goes away, and immediately forgets what kind of man he was. 25 But he who looks into the perfect law of liberty and continues in it, and is not a forgetful hearer but a doer of the work, this one will be blessed in what he does.

26 If anyone among you thinks he is religious, and does not bridle his tongue but deceives his own heart, this one's religion is useless. 27 Pure and undefiled religion before God and the Father is this: to visit orphans and widows in their trouble, and to keep oneself unspotted from the world. (NIV)

I believe GOD is speaking to us through James to tell us to tame our tongues. **I believe GOD is telling us that if we cannot control our tongues, our Bible study and church attendance and our giving are useless!** I thought of three quick responses that cause us to react with an **untamed tongue**:

1. Quick **defensive** response, trying to win or be superior.
2. Quick **insecure** response, trying to convince.
3. Quick **irrational** response, trying to support False Evidence Appearing Real (FEAR).

Responding quickly may not work like you think. You may be operating from **Limiting Beliefs**. For example:

1. To be heard, I need to respond quickly, emotionally and loudly.
2. Somebody has to lose in this discussion and it AIN'T gonna be me!
3. When I win and you lose, you will learn how to see things <u>my</u> way and life will be happy.

GOD wants us healed which makes our response more productive and filled with peace. A tamed tongue is required. Here is how:

James 1:19 *My dear brothers and sisters, take note of this: Everyone should be quick to listen, slow to speak and slow to become angry,*

1. **Hurry Up and Listen** – Repeat what the other person is saying to avoid misunderstanding.

2. **Use a Pregnant Pause** – This is an intentional 3 to 5 second pause to focus your thoughts on peace.
3. **Recognize and Be Above the Attack** – If this person is attacking, why should you? Remove the emotional response.

A controlled tongue takes practice. Add this and watch your conversations flourish.

Getting Unstuck

Unforgiveness keeps me stuck in a place that I do not want to be. Some people spend their entire lives in bondage because they refuse to forgive. Broken relationship after broken relationship could indicate there is some unforgiveness that needs to be achieved on your part. Can you think of people you no longer speak to? Will you be the bigger person and reach out to repair the relationship if it is salvageable? They may have moved beyond the offense or may not know how they offended you. Reconnecting with people will take courage and prayer for yourself and that person.

There is no logic behind unforgiveness, but I do understand it. I also understand and have experienced letting go of an attacker. **It is freeing to let go of an attacker!** You can let go of a person who wounds you and still connect with them every once in a while, in limited doses. For some, you may have to let them go permanently. Ask GOD if this offense should have you permanently separate yourself from this person. Pray for this person and let GOD do the rest.

WARNING

- Assess if you are operating from Fight Everyone Abolish Relationships (FEAR). Desiring to be the one who wins may inhibit everyone being restored. What does healthy restoration look like? Be careful of needing people to change in order to be around you or interact with you.
- Check how you handle pressure. If too many difficult situations come at you at once, do you lash out at people?

NEXT STEPS

- Slow your first reactions down enough to assess your defensiveness or woundedness.
- Pray for peaceful words and nonverbal expressions.
- Modify your expectations of other people by releasing the desire to see them change.
- Think in terms of **restoration**. GOD wants you fully restored and HE wants the same for your attacker. You may need to have the person restored from a distance if they cannot be restored in your life.
- If you still argue and fight, work on a plan to work together or release the person to GOD, praying for them to have the best, but self-examine your part in the argument to see if you have unforgiveness.

Can I reduce surprises by thinking ahead?

Be a Leader and Be Ready with Proactive Forgiveness

"You have been wounded." This is what doctors say to people who are in the hospital, because their bodies are injured and may be in shock. They may not feel that they are wounded, but they are. The same goes for leading your business when it comes to your woundedness. You may not think you are wounded but maybe you are. If you remain wounded, you can possibly carry those wounds into situations that need a healed person. You may think she is acting just like this other lady who caused you pain. Immediately the situation puts you back in the debilitating position of pain you may have experienced years or decades ago. GOD wants you healed.

Proactive Forgiveness is the act of preparing for potentially combative situations, arming yourself with peace, knowing you are not in control of the situation, and you have to trust GOD for outcomes.

Proactive Forgiveness takes maturity in Active Forgiveness and Reactive Forgiveness. In other words, you cannot be proactive in something you have not practiced.

> Leadership Tip #5 – Leaders are prepared for things to go wrong.

It took me years to find and reclaim my sense of identity after I was let go from a company by an attacker. My elevation to the top spots in a corporation caused me to lose touch with my giftedness in GOD, who created me for HIS purpose and for HIS glory. I thought I had to become what the company wanted me to be. If they said, "fire someone," I had to become "tough" enough to get rid of people. This was easy when the person was not performing, but the difficult times came when people who were performing well had to be laid off because of poor leadership decisions.

During the layoffs, I saw the same leaders who prompted the cuts protect themselves while others perished. After my corporate experience, when I saw what I thought was doubleminded, slanderous, or sneaky people, it made me remember how I was mistreated.

Overcoming Humiliation

In my last days as a leader of the large organization, I had to present a forecast for the upcoming year. Everyone I was presenting to began laughing, knowing that I would not be there to see anything in the forecast come to fruition. I felt humiliated!

I never wanted anyone to feel this type of humiliation. When I sensed humiliation would come from a person, I immediately practiced putting up a stone wall of protection between me and the person who reminded me of my humiliators. "*Before this person hurts me, I will protect myself,*" I thought to myself unknowingly. This seemed to work for a while, until I heard a sermon on the illusion of control. Are you trying to protect yourself by labeling people?

Illusion of Control

Trying to control situations caused me to lose trust in people. While I was regaining the confidence that was stolen, I did not realize my trust was stolen as well. I suspected people and my suspicions came true almost every time.

I felt good being able to finally see when someone was manipulating me or slandering me in front of people while smiling at me in my face. But GOD said to me, "It is not enough for you to know how wolf-like people can be; I want you to ask ME to forgive them."

This revelation was a gamechanger. Instead of bracing myself before I figuratively got hit by people, GOD wanted me to walk into situations, expecting that I will bring in HIS peace. Proactive Forgiveness helps me prepare to bring GOD's peace into situations, versus trying to figure out how to win the argument.

This helped me become a better servant leader. I still get angry and I still get enraged. But going into situations with Proactive Forgiveness helps me keep my head when I would otherwise lose it.

Time had to show me that GOD is in control. Over time, my enemies were let go from their respective companies. Yes, I said companies. I ran into bullies in other companies. They would be given a title and a little money and felt they had the right to mistreat people.

I wondered if I could ever reach a person who seemed dead set against me or my beliefs in GOD. **I had to learn to let go of people so they could self-discover JESUS as their daily guide and Savior, or not**. What is your heart towards people who remind you of your attacker?

GOD Sees Mistreatment

Little did they know that GOD saw every move. Every lie that was told, GOD heard. Every scale that was tipped unfairly was felt by GOD. The bullies I encountered were seen by GOD and were allowed to rule for a minute. Satan is allowed this freedom as well. He is allowed to tempt you and me, lie about us and try to get us killed by those who have been influenced by him.

Leaders of block clubs, sports teams, companies, cities or nations can fall to the influence of Satan. All of us have sinned, but some have given into that sin and want to harm other people. They demand harsh performance or be fired. Respect no longer exists amongst those who want to mistreat people and following GOD seems like more of a chore than a privilege to them.

Proactive Forgiveness takes into account, that the world will have persecutors. JESUS said in Matthew 5: 10 – 11 –

"[10] Blessed are those who are persecuted for righteousness' sake,
For theirs is the kingdom of heaven.

[11] Blessed are you when they revile and persecute you, and say all kinds of evil against you falsely for My sake. [12] Rejoice and be exceedingly glad, for great is your reward in heaven, for so they persecuted the prophets who were before you."

You Are Being Prepared

I believe HE is preparing us for the world's persecutors. I also do not think HE wants us to look forward to being persecuted. HE is preparing us and gives us a mindset that we should embrace. GOD saw the actions of the prophets and has a special reward for their service to HIM.

HE sees you and me being persecuted and has that same reward for us. HE also prepares us to be HIS leader instead of being the world's leader. Someone told me that the best leader has been fired or lost a business. I thought this was not true, until I heard about leaders who successfully came and went from companies. Some of these leaders got better and better each time they were let go. I feel the same way.

CHRIST Is the Best Example of a Leader

I was so busy becoming what worldly leaders expected, that I forgot what it was like to be what GOD expected. GOD wants me to be a leader who is C.H.R.I.S. and T. **C**ourageous, caring and compassionate. HE wants me to be **H**onest and humble. **R**espectful and reverent. **I**nteresting and intuitive. **S**aved and sent. **T**eachable and talented. In other words, HE wants me to be like HIM.

In the *GOD-Centered Business: A Foundational Framework to Grow with Resilience*, I supply a 36-Day daily devotional to study examples of leadership, CHRIST displayed.

Proactive Forgiveness helps me see the world differently. JESUS sees people in their forgiven state. In the middle of my sins, CHRIST died for me. HE forgave me before I was created.

I can have the fuel to go out into the world with resilience. I may still get wounded, but GOD has enabled me to let go of people and to stop trying to control their outcome. Have you considered the love JESUS has for you?

WARNING

- Assess if you are operating from False Evidence Appearing Real (FEAR).

NEXT STEPS

- Place peace in potential combative situations.
- Practice your statements of diffusing the situation versus escalating it.
- Be the first to forgive, apologize and show people a higher way of thinking, namely peaceably.
- Be strong, brave and courageous enough to reduce unnecessary fighting. You do not have to be a pushover when a bully attacks, but are you labeling people as an attacker because they remind you of previous attackers? Is this attack worth severing the relationship?

What does grace for myself look like?

Forgiving Myself to Become a Leader

Becoming what the company wanted me to be changed my perspective. I wanted the title and power to "help" the poor and overlooked. I was not prepared to have to do someone's dirty work. The higher I climbed, the more I was told to put a person in a position that did not have the expertise or charisma to perform the position. I had to get rid of good people to move in, what I thought, were bad people and put them in their place.

I was told I had to become tough. Little did I know, that the tougher I got, the more I became like the world. Humans praise leaders who do not mind hurting other humans. I am not talking about the fight between good and evil, I am speaking about those who believe that only the strong survive.

Only the Strong Survive Mindset

They spend time seeking who they can devour. With rage and force, they take and never give. They do this in pursuit of money. Others are motivated by becoming superior. Still others do it out of hatred. Whatever the motive, there were people who actively sought to receive power over people and I was becoming just like them.

Leadership Tip #6 – The gifts GOD gave you are valuable for your leadership.

GOD says through Paul in Romans 12:2 –

"And do not be conformed to this world, but be transformed by the renewing of your mind, that you may prove what is that good and acceptable and perfect will of God."

I Was Becoming Less of GOD's Leader

I was becoming more and more like the world without knowing it. I was impatient. This was a celebrated trait in the corporate world. I would give vendors deadlines, then quickly drop the vendor if they slipped even a day beyond the deadline. The company celebrated, but now this impatience was part of me and it came home with me, and my family had to experience it.

I could not travel well. When I saw someone fumbling in front of me, I would lose my patience instead of helping. Praying for people never crossed my mind as I watched the slow people act confused and bothersome!

I also became title driven. I treated people with respect, but I became wrapped up in "my" title. This was pride. Before I was laid off, I did not mind sharing that I worked at a large company and had a large responsibility. I felt like I fit in anywhere. But when I left the company, I felt ashamed when people asked me "what do you do?"

I had put my entire identity into the company that gave me lavish vacations, bonuses and stock options. I spoke day and night about the company because I felt that is what it took to climb the ladder. I was gaining the world and losing my soul.

JESUS said in Matthew 16:26 –

"For what profit is it to a man if he gains the whole world, and loses his own soul? Or what will a man give in exchange for his soul?"

I believe JESUS is not saying that HE only loves poor people, but HE warns rich, wealth minded people that they may be gaining power and losing their relationship with GOD. That is what I was doing.

Eventually, I found myself not being able to talk to someone about CHRIST like I used to. After years of not street witnessing, I decided to speak to someone at a furniture store about CHRIST. It was a disaster. I had no compassion, no prayer and possibly no result. I could feel it. How is the world changing you?

My Spiritual Connection Felt Broken

It felt like the spirit was gone. I am not speaking about the HOLY SPIRIT leaving; I am speaking about my spiritual connection to GOD as my leader felt gone. I was so much like the world, that when I opened my mouth for CHRIST, I sounded like the world. I was saved but no longer did I surrender my life to CHRIST.

I sat alone wondering where things had gone so wrong. My attacker got me out of what I thought was a great position, but in reality, I had become something that only the world appreciated. I felt that GOD did not even want me. But I was looking at myself through the world's eyes.

I had to forgive myself.

Importance of Self-Forgiveness

Forgiving yourself is important. The world will tell you how terrible you are and if you listen to it long enough, you may start to believe it. **Soon <u>the attacker becomes you</u> as you attack yourself with blame**. But GOD sees you differently. He sees you as a wonderful, beautiful, bright, salt-filled leader. You are salt. You are light. JESUS said so!

I made mistakes and you may have as well. Becoming insecure about those mistakes can lead to covering the mistakes up. Instead of shouting the mistake from the mountaintop, you hide it in the ground. GOD sees the hidden mistakes and then may ask you "What have you done with MY talent I gave you?" See the Parable of the Talents in Matthew 25 for more context.

The talent in this instance is the opportunity to share how you overcame a mistake instead of hiding it The more practice you have in hiding mistakes, the better you become at it.

Hidden Mistakes

Unfortunately, GOD sees the hidden mistake and wanted you to use it to bring people closer to CHRIST, but you didn't. You still can. But realize, <u>you are still forgiven if you cannot admit your mistake to other people but only to GOD</u>. It takes courage to open your mouth and tell people about the mistakes you made. Not every audience can hear every mistake you ever made, but you cannot keep this inside. The more you hide, the more you may not like yourself, the more you may not like other people and the more you may not like GOD. You may even blame HIM for being good and sovereign.

This becomes a slippery slope that is hard to impossible to recover from. GOD wants you and me to **use Active Forgiveness** on ourselves so we can have the capability to forgive others.

JESUS said in Matthew 6:15 –

"*But if you do not forgive men their trespasses, neither will your Father forgive your trespasses.*"

I believe JESUS means that we need to forgive ourselves and forgive other people. We do not have to be so hard on ourselves to "feel" forgiven, we "are" forgiven! 1 John 1:9 – "*If we confess our sins, He is faithful and just to forgive us our sins and to cleanse us from all unrighteousness.*" Confess and be forgiven.

WARNING

- Replaying your own faults is a tactic of the enemy. Know that GOD convicts you once, but Satan replays old wounds over and over, trying to keep you stuck.

NEXT STEPS

- Ask GOD to forgive you and be done with it.
- Even if you repeat the sin, know that GOD is willing to forgive you over and over and over.
- Look at other people differently and see each as GOD sees them.
- Fill your heart with love as a weapon.

Can I find peace?

Regaining Stolen Sleep

Leaders need rest. GOD gave us this example when HE created the world and rested on the seventh day. But what happens when you lay awake at night, brooding over what someone did to you? You may need a process to regain stolen sleep as prescribed in *GOD-Centered Business: A Foundational Framework to Grow with Resilience.*

How to regain lost sleep and peace

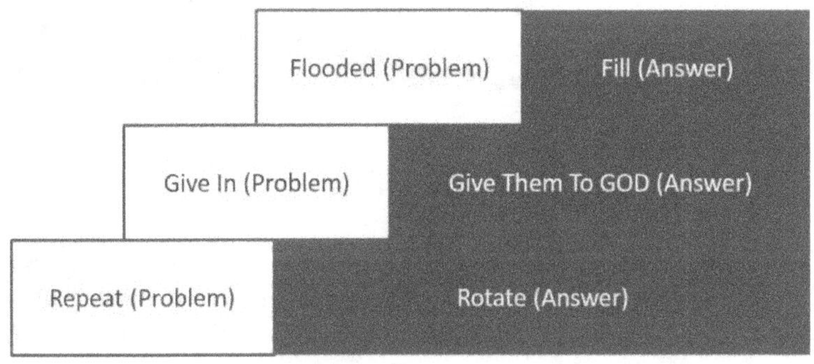

When someone has hurt you, three things can happen.
1. You repeat the hurt over and over trying to resolve the issue as best you can.
2. You give into a wrong solution which is usually a fight or hatred or fall prey to an addiction like alcohol, drugs or porn.
3. You carry the hurt to other situations and become hypersensitive to the hurt others are doing, therefore becoming flooded.

Have you ever lost sleep over the hurt someone imposed on you?

As a GOD-Centered business owner, you cannot afford to lose sleep. So how can we deal with the pain? R-G-F.

Rotate – Give – Fill Methodology to Regain Sleep

How to regain lost sleep and peace – Rotate Your Thinking to GOD

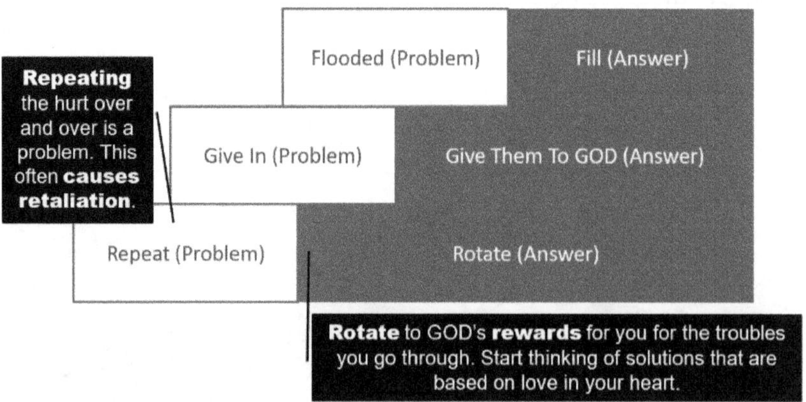

The first method of letting go of the pain is to R-Rotate. When you keep replaying a problem over and over in your head, you can get stuck and even worse, it can cause you to experience fear, anxiety and depression.

<u>Rotate</u> your thinking to what GOD wants you to think about.

Philippians 4:8 *Finally, brothers and sisters, whatever is true, whatever is noble, whatever is right, whatever is pure, whatever is lovely, whatever is admirable–if anything is excellent or praiseworthy–think about such things.*(NIV).

When do you have the best ideas? Is it when you love to do something or when you hate doing something? Instead of retaliation, can you rotate to love as your weapon and approach? Instead of writing that nasty note, practice asking GOD to bless the person with HIS love and forgiveness. Fill your heart with love and watch the power flood back into you. This will take practice.

– Romans 12:14-16 *Ask God to bless those who persecute you—yes, ask him to bless, not to curse. Be happy with those who are happy, weep with those who weep. Have the same concern for everyone. Do not be proud, but accept humble duties. Do not think of yourselves as wise.*

Blessing people releases bitterness from your heart. Rotating to a loving plan enables you to be above the situation.

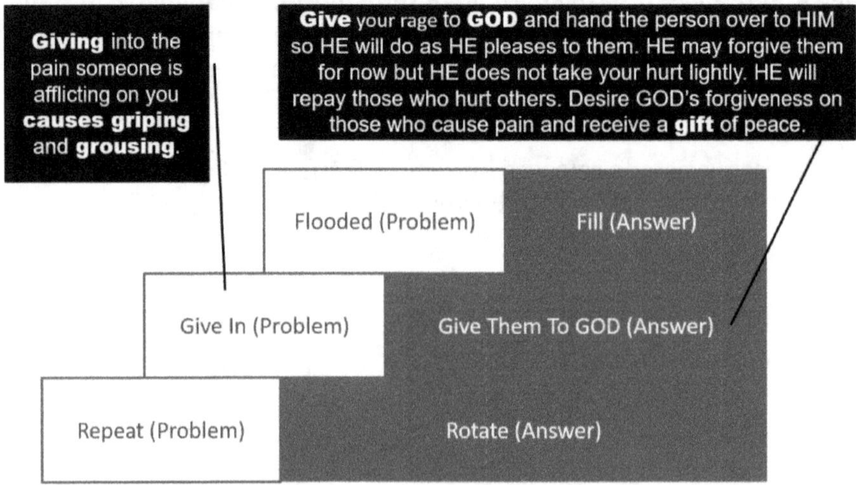

The next method to regain sleep and peace is to **G-Give** the person over to GOD. This means releasing the thought of getting revenge. Get off the dangerous path of trying to win the argument or trying to hurt them back.

Romans 12:18 – 19 *Do everything possible on your part to live in peace with everybody. Never take revenge, my friends, but instead let God's anger do it. For the scripture says, "I will take revenge, I will pay back, says the Lord."* (GNT)

Do you have anyone you can ask GOD to forgive?

Grow in grace by **G-<u>Giving</u>** them to GOD. Ask the LORD to have mercy on the person and then ask for GOD to have mercy on you. This takes practice.

Story of a man who loved GOD more than retaliation
There was a man who GOD loved very much. He chose to use love as a weapon instead of using retaliation. When his employer tried to kill him, he did not retaliate. Instead, he showed love. Everyone

knew this person would someday become the boss. They even told him, "You will rule someday."

That person is David, a man after GOD's own heart.

When King Saul tried to kill David, recorded in 1 Samuel 19, David did not retaliate because he knew he would someday be the king and chose to use love versus hate. He was above the situation. You can be above the situation.

You can read about David in the book of 1 Samuel.

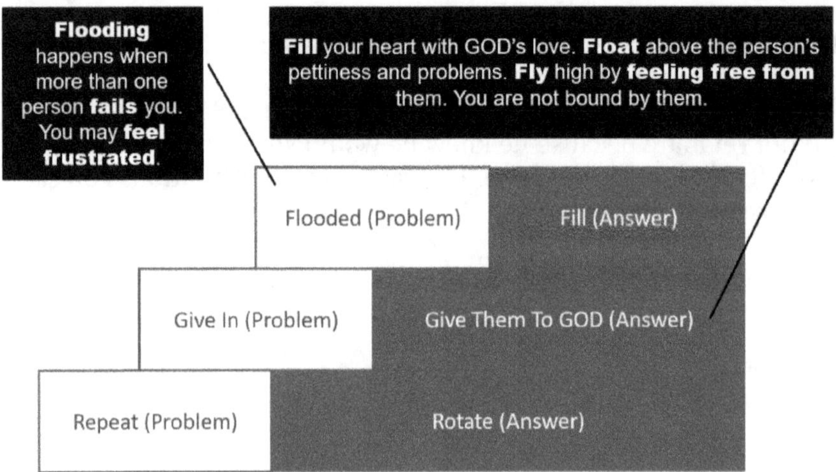

The last method to regaining peace and sleep is to **F-Fill** your heart with love. The person causing pain may be trying to rob you of peace. This can provoke you into anger and rage. Reduce the rage and fill your heart with love for them.

Love provides freedom they may be trying to steal from you.

Luke 6:27-36. "*But to you who are listening I Love your enemies, do good to those who hate you, bless those who curse you, pray for those who mistreat you. If someone slaps you on one cheek, turn to them the other also. If someone takes your coat, do not withhold your shirt from them. Give to everyone who asks you, and if anyone takes what belongs to you, do not demand it back. Do to others as you would have them do to you.*

"If you love those who love you, what credit is that to you? Even sinners love those who love them. And if you do good to those who are good to you, what credit is that to you? Even sinners do that. And if you lend to those from whom you expect repayment, what credit is that to you? Even sinners lend to sinners, expecting to be repaid in full. But love your enemies, do good to them, and lend to

them without expecting to get anything back. Then your reward will be great, and you will be children of the Most High, because he is kind to the ungrateful and wicked. Be merciful, just as your Father is merciful.

GOD is not saying become a wimp, rather be strong enough to choose love over petty retaliation. **You are a leader** who is above the situation. **You are bigger than this**. Your leadership in the area of forgiveness is necessary. The more people you can release, the more successful you can be. Using RGF, Rotate, Give, and Fill, enables you to focus on love for the person, giving vengeance to GOD and filling your heart with love and genuine concern for people. You will have peace.

WARNING

- Know that letting go takes practice. It feels good to be in control, but that control may be what is making you lose sleep.

NEXT STEPS

- Ask GOD to help you trust in HIS plan.
- Ask yourself, "Why am I not trusting GOD to handle this situation?"
- Schedule time on your calendar to think about the things that worry you. Limit this to a single day or hour.
- Place your worries in front of GOD and for each worry, give HIM praise.

Wanted

Leaders with courage.

Final Step to Leadership; Ask for Forgiveness

World leaders are told to never admit guilt because it shows weakness. This trickles down to national leaders, state leaders, city leaders, business owners, team leaders and perhaps you.

Good reasons are given to not admit guilt for doing something wrong. Public panic may set in or the stock of the company may fall or the church may close. But GOD does something strange to leaders who cannot admit when they are wrong. HE lets them think they got away with the act and lets their heart harden away from HIM.

Person 1 – Have you ever experienced a salesperson at a store who received your complaint well? Think of a time when the salesperson listened attentively and then apologized for the issue. How did she make you feel?

Person 2 – Have you ever experienced a salesperson who blamed you for the problem she caused? How did you feel about their attitude?

Between the two people, which one showed more leadership to you?

Real Leadership

Ask for forgiveness as an act of leadership.

Matthew 5:24 – *leave your gift there before the altar, and go your way. First be reconciled to your brother, and then come and offer your gift.*

> Leadership Tip #7 – Courage looks different to GOD. HIS leaders love and serve.

Leaders know that forgiveness is more important than being right. By seeking to be right, blame inserts itself into the heart and blinds the leader causing a failure. By seeking forgiveness, the blindness is lifted and the heart becomes cleansed and healed.

Courage Is Needed

Ask for Forgiveness

Courage to ask for forgiveness is needed right now from you.

Ask GOD for the courage to admit when they have wronged someone.

I have hurt the following people (Finish the sentence)
This is the way I hurt them (Finish the sentence)
I accept the power of forgiveness by asking JESUS and the following people for forgiveness:

It takes **courage** to run a business.

The skill of having courage is acquired when you forgive people and when you ask for forgiveness. Seeking forgiveness from a leadership role may be new to you but very familiar to others. Let's explore how to ask for forgiveness.

Let Go of Pride

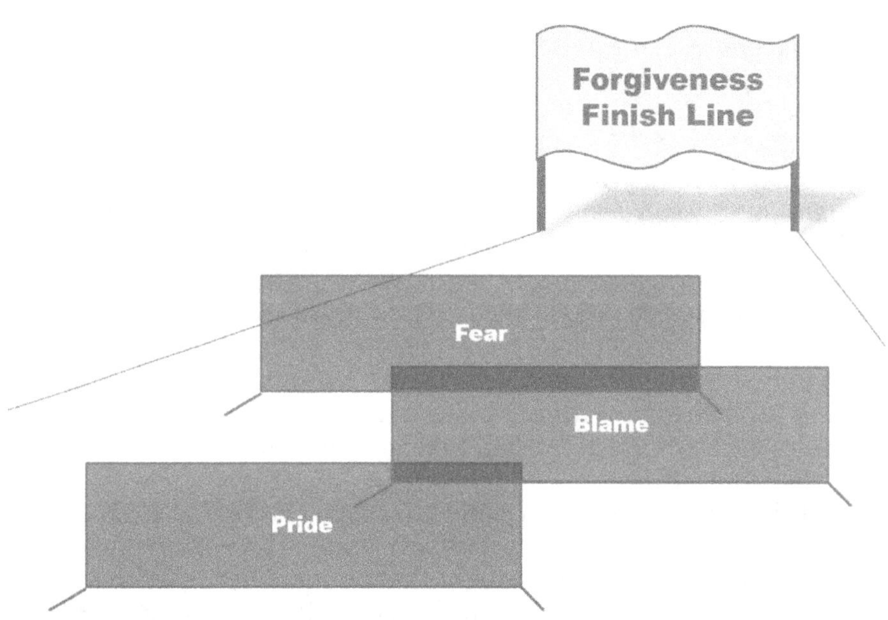

Asking for forgiveness can be just as hard, if not harder, than forgiving others. Here, you are relinquishing power and becoming vulnerable. There are many blockers to asking for forgiveness, but these three truly hurt your leadership.

Pride blocks you from thinking you need to ask for forgiveness.

Look at Satan's pride by reading out loud Isaiah 14: 13-15 *You said in your heart,*
"I will ascend to the heavens;
I will raise my throne
above the stars of God;
I will sit enthroned on the mount of assembly,
on the utmost heights of Mount Zaphon.
I will ascend above the tops of the clouds;

I will make myself like the Most High."
But you are brought down to the realm of the dead,
to the depths of the pit. (NIV)

Blame blocks you from necessary admission of guilt. Romans 2:1 *You, therefore, have no excuse, you who pass judgment on someone else, for at whatever point you judge another, you are condemning yourself, because you who pass judgment do the same things.*

Fear blocks you from growing as a leader. Matthew 16:24 --27 : *Then Jesus said to his disciples, "Whoever wants to be my disciple must deny themselves and take up their cross and follow me. For whoever wants to save their life will lose it, but whoever loses their life for me will find it. What good will it be for someone to gain the whole world, yet forfeit their soul? Or what can anyone give in exchange for their soul? For the Son of Man is going to come in his Father's glory with his angels, and then he will reward each person according to what they have done.*

Pride was Satan's main problem. Do you know that if Satan asked for forgiveness, he may not have gotten thrown out of heaven? Instead, he stuck with the thought that he could be higher than GOD. He thought he could control his own life rather than surrender it.

Blame was the problem Paul wrote about in Romans 2:1. Whenever the leader blames other people, it never looks good. Blame is detestable to GOD. HE wants people who are strong enough to admit wrong.

Fear causes people to self-protect. You spend most of the day worrying about bills, making more money and what it would be like to have more and more. You never once ask GOD, "What do YOU want to do with my life?" GOD wants you to let go of your life so it can be saved. The more fearful control you have, the less GOD can work through you.

Do you have pride or blame or fear? If so, what can you do about it?

Answer to Pride Is Appreciation

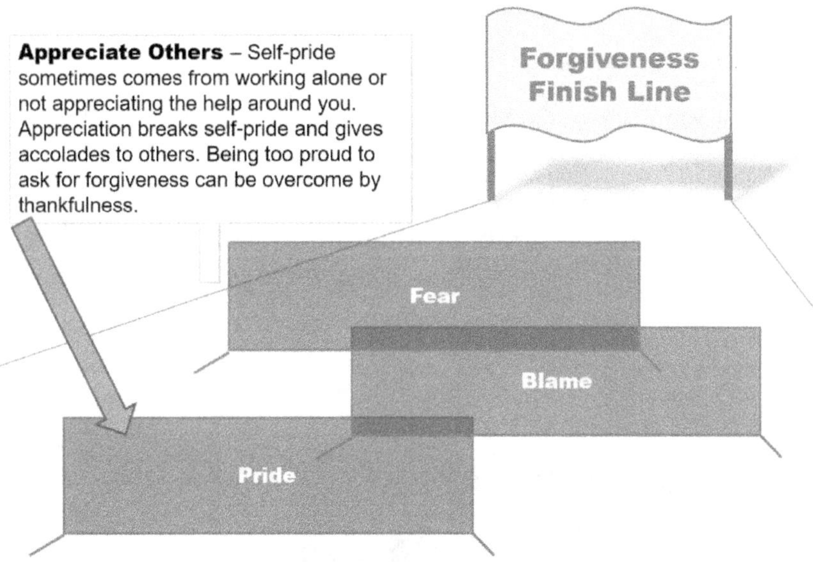

Appreciation erases harmful pride. If you are too proud to approach the person you harmed to ask for forgiveness, then it will affect other relationships. It is a heart thing that cannot be masked.

Fill your heart with appreciation for him or her. See them as GOD sees and values people. They deserve a sincere apology.

Answer to Blame Is Accepting Responsibility

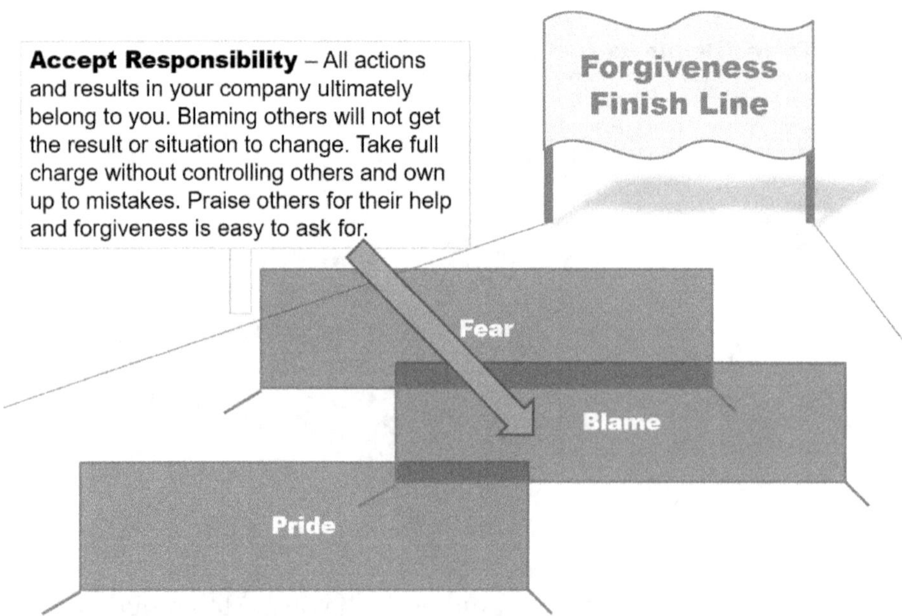

Have you ever asked a kid who clearly broke your stuff, "What happened?" How do kids respond if they are guilty and don't want you to show their guilt?

Accepting responsibility is a must for the GOD-Centered Business owner. Leaders who own the mistakes of their employees and sometimes their customers, shine brighter than people who blame.

Answer to Fear Is Abbreviated Time Alone

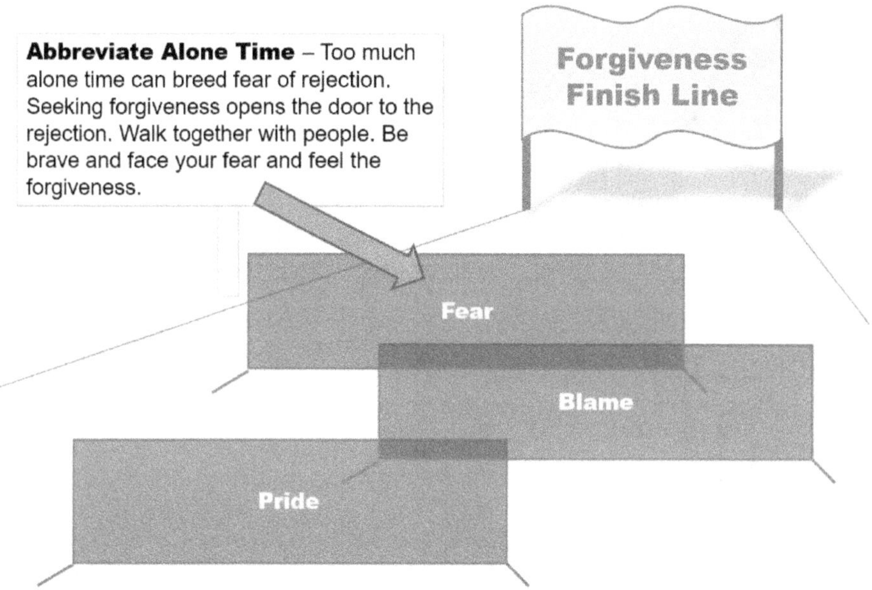

Have you ever said, "Well I don't need them anyway?" How many times can you say this until you are alone?

Abbreviate alone time to rid yourself of fear. This is your group who will be there for you to help face fears and to talk about problems. Some of you may enjoy being alone, but if you have fear, it is best to be with a group to help you.

This fear that some people face may cause them to be too scared to ask for forgiveness. "What if the truth comes out?" you might ask. Good, then now you are free.

GOD wants you to be free, so ask HIM for the courage to admit wrong.

When JESUS forgives, it is permanent. HE saw every sin you and I did, yet HE died for us and took the blame anyway. When HE rose from the dead, HE received all authority to forgive, pardon and make people right with HIM.

WARNING

- Do not give into the enemy's attack of trying to keep you from truly healing. Uncover the hidden thing, no matter how long it has been hidden.

NEXT STEPS

- Ask people for forgiveness.
- Appreciate people.
- Accept responsibility.
- Abbreviate walking alone.

Prayers to Regain My Leadership

Dear LORD help me to forgive one of YOUR children. I still remember what was done and I desire to let go. Please give this person the best, which is YOUR SON. I give them over to YOU to do as YOU wish. I forgive them. They have no more power over me. YOU have all the power! I do not have to see them get converted, rather I need YOU to repair my sleep. Repair my pain. Repair my sense of identity. Please restore me in abundance with joy and trust. Please do not let unforgiveness hold me back. Amen.

Dear LORD please help me to speak slower and to relax my obvious dissatisfied emotions right now. The emotion I feel is correct, but I want my response to be aligned with YOUR peace. LORD, tame my tongue right now so I can speak words of peace to help us all work together. Help me to forgive the words that were just said. Help me step away from this conversation for a moment to hear YOUR guidance. Is this the situation that will separate us? Or is this the situation that sheds light into the problem with our relationship? Please give me discernment. Amen.

Dear LORD, here I am again about to walk into the same situation I have been in before. Please protect me from any harm that someone has planned for me. LORD, please forgive those who plan harm to fall on me and open their eyes to YOUR love. Let this situation go without incidents and make our path straight. Give us this day our daily bread. And forgive us our debts as we forgive our debtors. Thank YOU for what YOU are going to do in advance. Amen.

Dear LORD, please forgive me. YOU know exactly what I have done and when I did it and how I did it. I confess what I did, and I need YOU to cleanse me of all unrighteousness. Please restore me and give me a new way of thinking. I want to grow up. Amen.

In JESUS name amen!

About the Author

Stan Washington is a teacher of the Bible, not a preacher. He accepted the LORD at the age of 12. He walked away from serving GOD in college and pursued fulfilling his own desires. His pursuit led him to barely finish college. He became a programmer but wanted to get into learning about the business world. Still empty, he returned to the LORD wanting to get his life in order. He took many continuing education classes at a Bible Institute.

Later, he joined the largest quick service restaurant and became a McDonald's executive over Operations and Technology. After many years he turned to entrepreneurism and became the founder and president of Honor Services Office, a software company that helps small businesses grow in CHRIST as they grow their business. He is ready to share the tips he learned from his experiences while enabling a community of prayer to truly follow JESUS. Stan is the author of *GOD-Centered Business: A Foundational Framework to Grow with Resilience* and also is the co-author of *Plans to Prosper: Strategies, Systems and Tools for Small Business Marketing Success.*

He is married and has two children. He has traveled to Zimbabwe, China, Mexico, and many places in the United States to spread the great news about JESUS.

Contact us:

Facebook: @HonorServicesOffice and GOD-Centered Business: Global People of All Colors

LinkedIn: Honor Services God Centered Business

Instagram : **@HonorServicesOffice**

https://www.HonorServicesOffice.com

YouTube: https://www.youtube.com/@honorservicesoffice

Author's Daily Devotional *(This is my quiet time)*
https://www.facebook.com/groups/honordevotional

https://honordevotional.blogspot.com

Other Do it Yourself Resources

Here are some other resources you can leverage to help grow your business:

Business Foundation

This study guide includes visioning, resilience testing, marketing, sales and customer service tips and a 36-day devotional.

***GOD-Centered Business: A Foundational Framework to Grow with Resilience Copyright 2020 ISBN:* 978-0-9909831-6-3**

GOD-Centered Business Presentation

There is also a presentation that goes with the class. The presentation is for use with the GOD-centered Business class and can be downloaded from www.honorservices office.com. Feel free to use this in print or presentation format.

Marketing Growth Tools

***Plans to Prosper: Strategies, Systems and Tools for Small Business Marketing Success (Victoria Cook and Stan Washington) Copyright 2015 ISBN:* 978-0-9909831-0-1**

Business Management Software

Honor Services Office is a small business management tool that provides an easy to use CRM, Online invoice / Bookkeeping System and Content Marketing system.

***Visit* https://www.HonorServicesOffice.com**

www.ingramcontent.com/pod-product-compliance
Lightning Source LLC
LaVergne TN
LVHW010939110826
845149LV00013B/2673
* 9 7 8 0 9 9 0 9 8 3 1 7 0 *